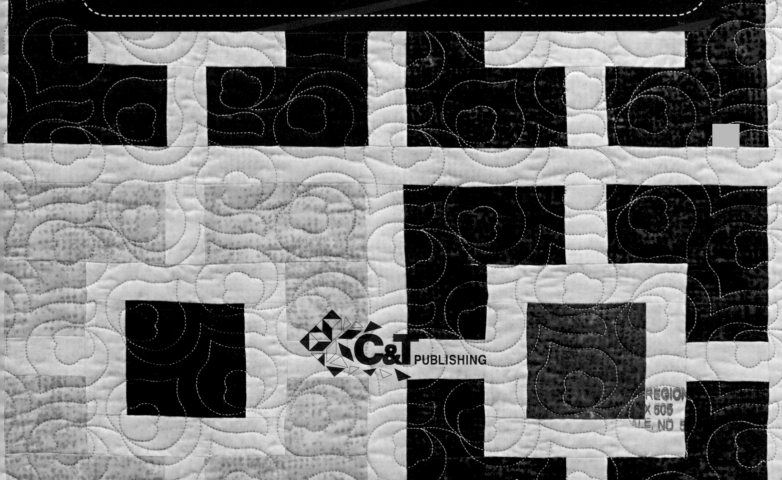

A Merry Christmas

with Kim Schaefer

27 Festive Projects to Deck Your Home
Quilts, Tree Skirts, Wreaths & More

Kim Schaefer

C&T PUBLISHING

Text copyright © 2015 by Kim Schaefer

Photography and artwork copyright © 2015 by C&T Publishing, Inc.

Publisher: Amy Marson

Creative Director: Gailen Runge

Art Director: Kristy Zacharias

Editor: Lynn Koolish

Technical Editors: Helen Frost and Debbie Rodgers

Cover Designers: Christina Jarumay Fox and April Mostek

Book Designer: April Mostek

Production Coordinator: Jenny Davis

Production Editor: Joanna Burgarino

Illustrators: Zinnia Heinzmann and Freesia Pearson Blizard

Photo Assistant: Mary Peyton Peppo

Style photography by Nissa Brehmer and instructional photography by Diane Pedersen, unless otherwise noted

Published by C&T Publishing, Inc., P.O. Box 1456, Lafayette, CA 94549

Library of Congress Cataloging-in-Publication Data

Schaefer, Kim, 1960-

 A Merry Christmas with Kim Schaefer : -27 festive projects to deck your home - quilts, tree skirts, wreaths & more / Kim Schaefer.

   pages cm

 ISBN 978-1-61745-045-7 (soft cover)

 1. Quilting--Patterns. 2. Quilted goods. 3. House furnishings. 4. Christmas decorations. I. Title.

 TT835.S28427 2015

 746.46--dc23

                  2014036809

Printed in China

10 9 8 7 6 5 4 3 2 1

Acknowledgments

I am so blessed to be part of the C&T family. Thanks to all of you for your continued support and dedication to publishing the best books possible.

Special thanks to:

Lynn Koolish—*my favorite editor*

Helen Frost—*the best technical editor*

Diane Minkley—*my very own longarm quilter*

Contents

Introduction   7

General Instructions   8
Rotary Cutting • Piecing • Pressing • Appliqué • Putting It All Together • Layering the Quilt • Quilting • Color and Fabric Choices • Yardage and Fabric Requirements

Projects   **10**

Tree Skirts

The Christmas Line   12
Kaleidoscope   14
Totally Square   16

Place Mats   18
Snowman • Reindeer • Santa Sidebar • Ornament • Woven

Kaleidoscope Tree Skirt

Table Toppers

Ornament   24
Confetti   28

Runners

Dots and Stripes   30
Holiday   32

Ornament Place Mat

Quilts

Losing My Head Wall Quilt   34
The Christmas Line Wall Quilt   36
Double Wrap Lap Quilt   38

Wreaths

Ornament   42

Holly Berry   44

Banners

Merry Christmas   46

Happy Holidays   48

Coasters   50

Peppermint • Snowflake • Holly • Snowman
Tree • Bird • Lines • Pieced

Gift Tags   54

Holly • Santa • Snowman • Tree
Ornament • Reindeer • Bird • Snowflake

Pillows

Squares   57

Patched   58

Side Stripes   59

Quilted Circles   60

Ornament Tree   61

About the Author   63

Holly Berry Wreath

Pieced Coaster

Side Stripes Pillow

A Merry Christmas with Kim Schaefer

Introduction

Christmas is a special time of year, filled with warm memories, honored traditions, and cherished time spent with family and friends. So many of my fondest memories are centered around the holiday season. A tradition that continues to bring me joy is that of making handmade projects for the holidays.

This book contains a variety of projects, including tree skirts, pillows, banners, wall quilts, table toppers, runners, place mats, coasters, gift tags, and more—all perfect for decorating your home or to give as gifts. There are projects suitable for beginners and more experienced sewists alike.

I hope this collection of projects will inspire you to create some holiday magic of your own.

Enjoy the season!

Kim

General Instructions

Rotary Cutting

I recommend that you cut all the fabrics used in the pieced blocks, borders, and bindings with a rotary cutter, an acrylic ruler, and a cutting mat. Trim the blocks and borders with these tools as well.

Piecing

All piecing measurements include ¼″ seam allowances. If you sew an accurate ¼″ seam, you will succeed! My biggest and best quiltmaking tip is to learn to sew an accurate ¼″ seam.

Pressing

Press seams to one side, preferably toward the darker fabric. Press flat and avoid sliding the iron over the pieces, which can distort and stretch them. When you join two seamed sections, press the seams in opposite directions so you can nest the seams and reduce bulk.

Appliqué

All appliqué instructions are for paper-backed fusible web with machine appliqué, and all the patterns have been drawn in reverse. If you prefer a different appliqué method, you will need to trace a mirror image of the pattern and add seam allowances to the appliqué pieces. A lightweight paper-backed fusible web works best for machine appliqué. Choose your favorite fusible web and follow the manufacturer's directions.

General Appliqué Instructions

1. Trace all parts of the appliqué design on the paper side of the fusible web. Trace each layer of the design separately. Whenever two shapes in the design butt together, overlap them by about ⅛″ to help prevent a gap between them. When tracing the shapes, extend the underlapped edge ⅛″ beyond the drawn edge in the pattern. Write the pattern letter or number on each traced shape.

2. Cut around the appliqué shapes, leaving a ¼″ margin around each piece.

3. Iron each fusible web shape to the wrong side of the appropriate fabric, following the manufacturer's instructions for fusing. (I don't worry about the grainline when placing the pieces.) Cut on the traced lines and peel off the paper backing. A thin layer of fusible web will remain on the wrong side of the fabric. This layer will adhere the appliqué pieces to the backgrounds.

4. Position the pieces on the backgrounds. The pieces are numbered in appliqué order. Press to fuse them in place.

5. Machine stitch around the appliqué pieces using a zigzag, satin, or blanket stitch. Stitch any detail lines indicated on the patterns. My choice is the satin stitch. I generally use matching threads for all the stitching. As always, the type of stitching you use and the thread color you select are personal choices.

Putting It All Together

When all the pieces are completed for a wall quilt, lap quilt, or table runner, arrange them on the floor or, if you are lucky enough to have one, a design wall. Arrange and rearrange the pieces until you are happy with the overall look. Each project has specific directions, as well as diagrams and photos, for assembly.

Layering the Quilt

Cut the batting and backing pieces 4″–5″ larger than the quilt top. Place the pressed backing on the bottom, right side down. Place the batting over the backing and the quilt top on top, right side up. Make sure all the layers are flat and smooth and the quilt top is centered over the batting and backing. Pin or baste the quilt.

Note: If you are going to have your top quilted by a longarm quilter, contact your quilter for specific batting and backing requirements, as they may differ from the instructions above.

The pillow fronts and backs are quilted to the batting only. When finishing the tree skirts, leave the backing whole until the piece is quilted. Then trim the center and cut the opening at the rear of the skirt.

Quilting

Quilting is a personal choice; you may prefer hand or machine quilting. My favorite method is to send the quilt top to a longarm quilter. This method keeps my number of unfinished tops low and the number of finished quilts high.

Color and Fabric Choices

I used 100% cotton fabrics in the projects in this book. These fabrics are easy to work with and are readily available at your local quilt shop.

I have a very relaxed approach to color and fabric choices, and although I have been trained in color theory, I feel most of my choices are intuitive. I use a design wall and usually play with the fabrics before I sew them. I have found that, in general, the more fabrics I use in a quilt, the more I like it. If you are new to quilting or are feeling unsure of your color choices, that is something you, too, can try.

Thankfully everyone has different tastes and preferences when it comes to color. In the end, it is your quilt and your choice. What's most important is that it is visually pleasing to you.

Yardage and Fabric Requirements

I have given yardage and fabric requirements for each project, with many projects calling for a total amount of assorted fabrics that can be used as a base for your project. The yardage amounts may vary depending on the number of fabrics used and the number of pieces you cut from each fabric. Always cut the pieces for the patchwork first, then cut any appliqué pieces.

The amounts given for binding allow for 2″-wide strips cut on the straight of grain. I usually use the same fabric for backing and binding, as this is a good way to use leftover fabric. Cut the binding strips either on the crosswise or lengthwise grain of the leftover fabric—whichever will yield the longest strips.

I used bias binding for the oval place mats (Place Mats, page 18) and the Christmas Line Tree Skirt (page 12), as well as for the center openings on the Kaleidoscope Tree Skirt (page 14) and the Totally Square Tree Skirt (page 16).

PROJ

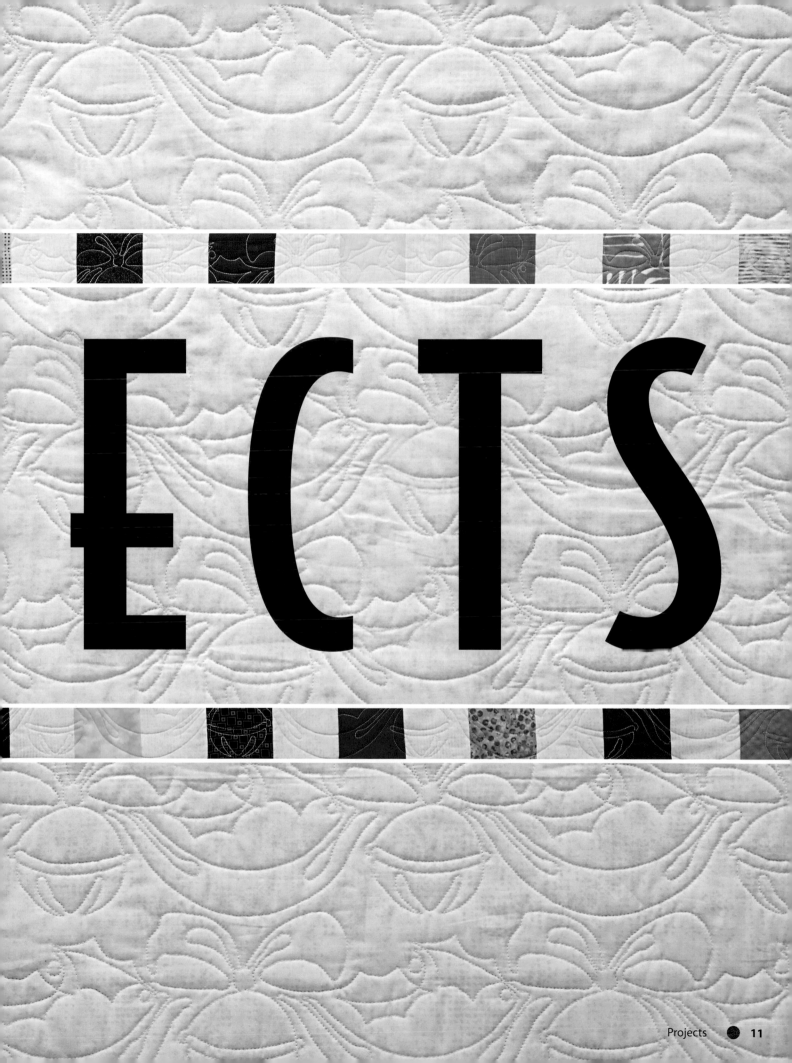

ECTS

The Christmas Line Tree Skirt

FINISHED TREE SKIRT SIZE: 56″ in diameter

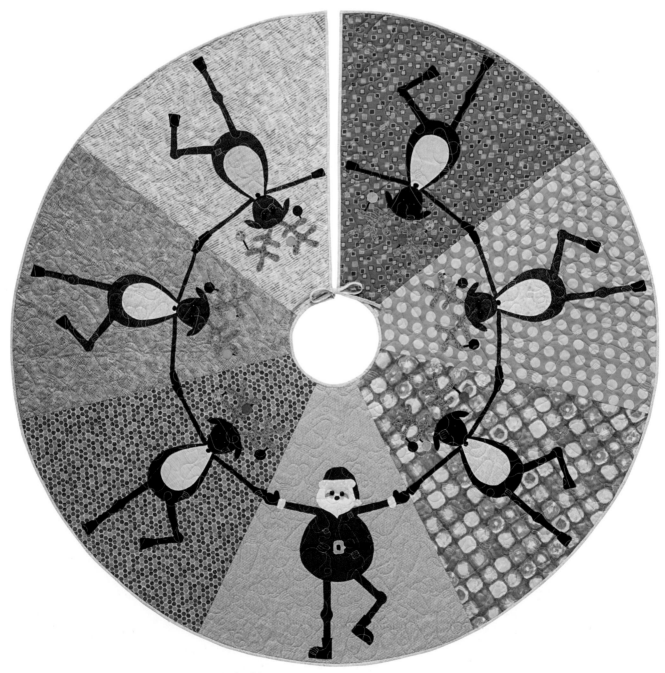

Quilted by Diane Minkley of Patched Works, Inc.

A Merry Christmas with Kim Schaefer

Santa and his reindeer will kick up their heels under the tree. This whimsical appliquéd tree skirt is sure to delight both the young and not so very young.

Materials

- ¾ yard each of 7 greens for appliqué backgrounds
- 6 fat quarters of assorted browns for reindeer
- ⅛ yard black for noses, bells, hooves, ornament hangers, mittens, belt, and boots
- ⅛ yard total assorted tans for bellies
- ⅛ yard tan for antlers
- 1 fat quarter of red for Santa suit
- Assorted scraps for ornaments, Santa face, beard, cheeks, and belt buckle
- 3 yards paper-backed fusible web
- 3½ yards for backing and binding
- 61″ × 61″ batting
- 14 small black buttons for eyes
- Plastic template material (4 sheets, 12″ × 18″)

Cutting

Pattern piece is on pullout page P3.

Staple the plastic template sheets together and make a template of pattern piece 1. Trace and cut 7 of pattern piece 1 for appliqué backgrounds, following the grainline arrow.

Appliquéing

Refer to Appliqué (page 8) as needed. Appliqué patterns are on pullout pages P1 and P3.

1. Using the appliqué patterns:

- Cut 6 each of appliqué pieces 2 through 9.
- Cut 18 of appliqué piece 10.
- Cut an ⅛″-wide strip into 18 pieces at assorted lengths for ornament hangers.
- Cut 1 each of appliqué pieces 11 through 28.

2. Refer to the panel diagrams (below) as you appliqué all the pieces, except the reindeer hand hooves and the Santa gloves and cuffs, to the backgrounds. *Note: I appliquéd each tree skirt panel individually, as they are easier to maneuver.*

Putting It All Together

1. Refer to the photo (page 12) as you sew together the tree skirt panels, leaving the rear seam unsewn.

2. Appliqué the hand hooves, gloves, and cuffs to the tree skirt.

Finishing

1. Layer the tree skirt with batting and backing. Baste or pin.

2. Quilt as desired and bind. (*Note: The outer and center circle binding must be cut on the bias.*) Bind the outer and open edges first; then bind the center opening, leaving 8″ to 10″ tails. Topstitch the tails to make ties.

3. Hand sew buttons for Santa and reindeer eyes.

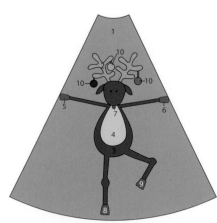

Reindeer panel   Santa panel

Kaleidoscope Tree Skirt

FINISHED TREE SKIRT SIZE: 51″ in diameter

Quilted by Diane Minkley of Patched Works, Inc.

This octagonal tree skirt is super simple to piece and looks great under the tree.

Materials

- 2¼ yards black print for center
- 1½ yards stripe for border
- 3⅛ yards for backing and binding
- 56″ × 56″ batting
- Plastic template material (3 sheets, 12″ × 18″)

Cutting

Pattern pieces are on pullout page P3.

Staple the plastic template sheets together and make a template of pattern pieces 1 and 2. Trace and cut 8 each of pattern pieces 1 and 2, following the grainline arrows.

Piecing

1. Refer to the putting it all together diagram (below) as you sew the border pieces to the center panels. Press.

2. Sew together the 8 panels, leaving the rear seam unsewn. Press.

Finishing

1. Layer the tree skirt with batting and backing. Baste or pin.

2. Quilt as desired and bind. *Note:* The center circle binding must be cut on the bias.

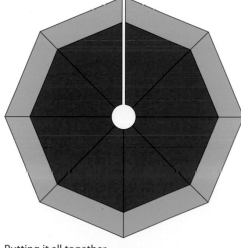

Putting it all together

Totally Square Tree Skirt

FINISHED TREE SKIRT SIZE: 48½″ × 48½″

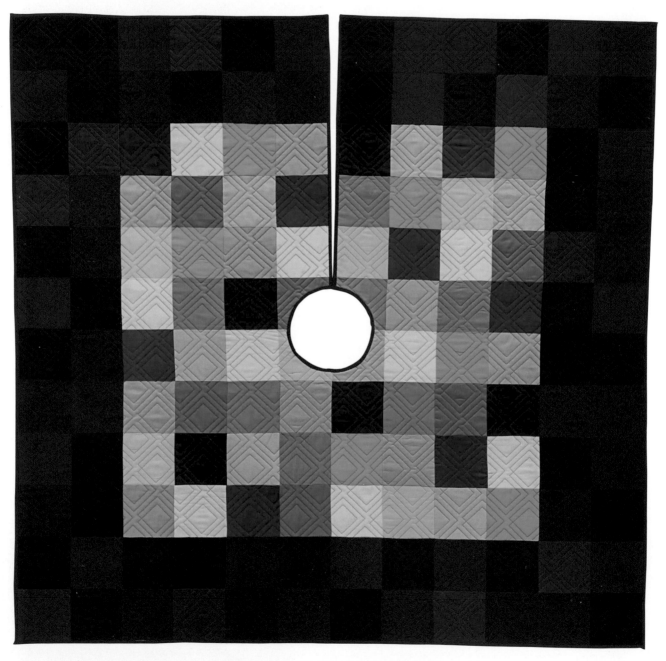

Quilted by Diane Minkley of Patched Works, Inc.

A Merry Christmas with Kim Schaefer

A kaleidoscope of red and green solids is created in this easy-to-piece contemporary tree skirt.

Materials

- 1¼ yards total assorted greens for pieced center

- 1½ yards total assorted reds for pieced outer borders

- 3⅛ yards for backing and binding

- 53″ × 53″ batting

- Plastic template of 6″ circle

Cutting

CUT FROM THE ASSORTED GREENS

64 squares 4½″ × 4½″ for the pieced center

CUT FROM THE ASSORTED REDS

80 squares 4½″ × 4½″ for the pieced borders

Piecing

1. Refer to the putting it all together diagram (below) as you arrange and sew together the squares in 12 rows of 6 squares each and 6 rows of 12 squares each. Join the rows, leaving the rear seam unsewn. Press.

2. Position the 6″ plastic template at the skirt center. Trace and cut on the drawn line for the center circle.

Finishing

1. Layer the tree skirt with batting and backing. Baste or pin.

2. Quilt as desired and bind. *Note:* The center circle binding must be cut on the bias.

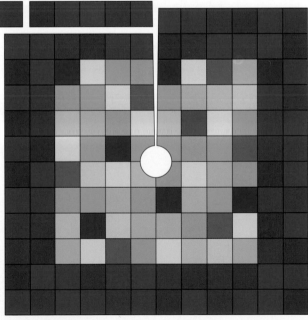

Putting it all together

Place Mats

Snowman Place Mat

FINISHED PLACE MAT SIZE: 18″ × 12½″ oval

Materials

- ¾ yard teal for background, backing, and bias binding
- ⅓ yard light for snowman head and shoulders
- ⅛ yard black for neck, arms, mouth, and eyes
- Scrap of orange for nose
- ½ yard paper-backed fusible web
- 22″ × 16″ batting

Cutting

Pattern pieces are on pullout page P1.

CUT FROM THE TEAL

2 of pattern piece 1 for the front and back

Appliquéing

*Refer to Appliqué (page 8) as needed.
Appliqué patterns are on pullout page P1.*

1. Using the appliqué patterns:

- Cut 1 each of appliqué pieces 2 through 8.
- Cut 2 of appliqué piece 9.

2. Refer to the putting it all together diagram (below) as you appliqué the pieces to the background.

Finishing

1. Layer the place mat with batting and backing. Baste or pin.

2. Quilt as desired and bind with bias binding.

Putting it all together

Mix and match a set of place mats for yourself or to give as a gift to someone special.

Reindeer Place Mat

FINISHED PLACE MAT SIZE: 18″ × 12½″ oval

Materials

- ¾ yard teal for background, backing, and bias binding
- ¼ yard brown for reindeer
- ⅛ yard tan for antlers
- Scrap of black for eyes
- Scrap of red for nose
- ½ yard paper-backed fusible web
- 22″ × 16″ batting

Cutting

Pattern pieces are on pullout page P2. Pattern piece 1 is included on the Snowman Place Mat pattern (pullout page P1).

CUT FROM THE TEAL

2 of pattern piece 1 for the front and back

Appliquéing

Refer to Appliqué (page 8) as needed. Appliqué patterns are on pullout page P2.

1. Using the appliqué patterns:

- Cut 1 each of appliqué pieces 2 through 5.
- Cut 2 of appliqué piece 6.

2. Refer to the putting it all together diagram (below) as you appliqué the pieces to the background.

Finishing

1. Layer the place mat with batting and backing. Baste or pin.

2. Quilt as desired and bind with bias binding.

Putting it all together

Santa Place Mat

FINISHED PLACE MAT SIZE: 18″ × 12½″ oval

Materials

- ¾ yard green for background, backing, and bias binding
- ¼ yard total assorted white-on-whites for beard, mustache, hat trim, and pom-pom
- ¼ yard tan for face
- ¼ yard red for hat
- Scrap of black for eyes
- Scrap of pink for cheeks
- Scrap of red for nose and mouth
- ¾ yard paper-backed fusible web
- 22″ × 16″ batting

Cutting

Pattern pieces are on pullout page P2. Pattern piece 1 is included on the Snowman Place Mat pattern (pullout page P1).

CUT FROM THE GREEN

2 of pattern piece 1 for the front and back

Appliquéing

Refer to Appliqué (page 8) as needed. Appliqué patterns are on pullout page P2.

1. Using the appliqué patterns:

- Cut 1 each of appliqué pieces 2 through 12.
- Cut 2 each of appliqué piece 13.

2. Refer to the putting it all together diagram (below) as you appliqué the pieces to the background.

Finishing

1. Layer the place mat with batting and backing. Baste or pin.

2. Quilt as desired and bind with bias binding.

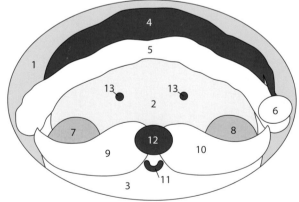

Putting it all together

Sidebar Place Mat

FINISHED PLACE MAT SIZE: 18½″ × 12½″

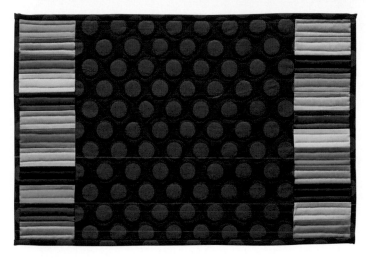

Materials

- 1 fat quarter of red dot for center
- ⅛ yard total assorted green solids for pieced rows
- 1 fat quarter for backing
- ¼ yard for binding
- 22″ × 16″ batting

Cutting

CUT FROM THE RED DOT

1 square 12½″ × 12½″ for the place mat center

CUT FROM THE ASSORTED GREEN SOLIDS

24 rectangles 1½″ × 3½″ for the pieced rows

Piecing

1. Refer to the putting it all together diagram (below) as you arrange and sew together 2 rows of 12 rectangles each. Press.

2. Join the rows and the center. Press.

Finishing

1. Layer the place mat with batting and backing. Baste or pin.

2. Quilt as desired and bind.

Putting it all together

Ornament Place Mat

FINISHED PLACE MAT SIZE: 18½″ × 12½″

Appliquéing

Refer to Appliqué (page 8) as needed. Appliqué patterns are on pullout page P3.

1. Using the appliqué patterns:

- Cut 3 each of appliqué piece 1.

- Cut 1 each of appliqué pieces 2, 3, and 4.

2. Refer to the putting it all together diagram (below) as you appliqué the pieces to the background.

Materials

- 1 fat quarter of green stripe for background

- ⅛ yard total assorted reds for ornaments

- ⅛ yard black for ornament hangers

- 1 fat quarter for backing

- ¼ yard for binding

- ⅛ yard paper-backed fusible web

- 22″ × 16″ batting

Finishing

1. Layer the place mat with batting and backing. Baste or pin.

2. Quilt as desired and bind.

Putting it all together

Cutting

CUT FROM THE GREEN STRIPE

1 rectangle 18½″ × 12½″

Woven Place Mat

FINISHED PLACE MAT SIZE: 18½″ × 12½″

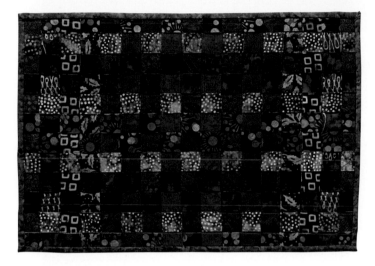

Materials

- ⅓ yard total assorted red batiks

- ⅔ yard total assorted green batiks

- 1 yard fast2fuse double-sided stiff fusible interfacing

- ¼ yard for binding

Cutting

CUT FROM THE RED BATIKS

22 strips 1″ × 12½″

CUT FROM THE GREEN BATIKS

12 strips 1″ × 12½″

24 strips 1″ × 18½″

CUT FROM THE FAST2FUSE

12 strips 1″ × 18½″

17 strips 1″ × 12½″

Putting It All Together

1. Sandwich the fast2fuse strips between the wrong sides of the batik strips. Press and fuse the fabric to the fast2fuse.

2. Refer to the photo (left) as you arrange and weave the strips together.

Finishing

Bind the place mat.

Ornament Table Topper

FINISHED BLOCK SIZE: 12″ × 12″ • **FINISHED TABLE TOPPER SIZE:** 40½″ × 40½″

Quilted by Diane Minkley of Patched Works, Inc.

Bring the festivities to the table with this fun pieced and appliquéd table topper.

Materials

- 1¼ yards total assorted reds for pieced center
- 1¼ yards green for outer border
- ½ yard total assorted brights for ornaments
- ⅛ yard black for ornament hangers
- 1¼ yards paper backed fusible web
- 45″ × 45″ batting
- 2⅝ yards for backing and binding

Cutting

Note: The pieces for each matching set of rectangles are listed together. Use 2 of each size for each block.

CUT FROM THE ASSORTED REDS

4 squares 2½″ × 2½″

8 rectangles 1½″ × 2½″ and 8 rectangles 1½″ × 4½″

8 rectangles 2½″ × 4½″ and 8 rectangles 2½″ × 8½″

8 rectangles 1½″ × 8½″ and 8 rectangles 1½″ × 10½″

8 rectangles 1½″ × 10½″ and 8 rectangles 1½″ × 12½″

CUT FROM THE GREEN

2 rectangles 8½″ × 24½″ for the 2 side borders

2 rectangles 8½″ × 40½″ for the top and bottom borders

Piecing

Make 4 blocks as shown. Press.

Step 1

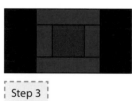

Step 2

Step 3

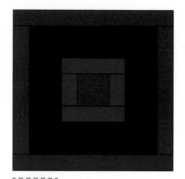

Step 6

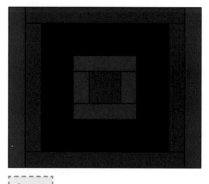

Step 7

Step 4

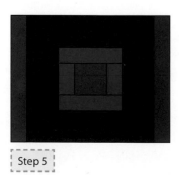

Step 5

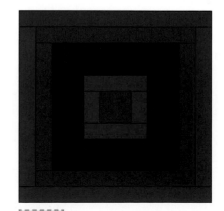

Step 8

Piecing

1. Refer to the block and border assembly diagram (right) as you arrange and sew together the blocks in 2 rows of 2 blocks each. Press.

2. Sew together the rows. Press.

3. Sew the 2 side borders to the table topper. Press.

4. Sew the top and bottom borders to the table topper. Press.

Appliquéing

Refer to Appliqué (page 8) as needed.
Appliqué patterns are on pullout page P4.

1. Using the appliqué patterns:

- Cut 12 of appliqué piece 1.
- Cut 8 of appliqué piece 2.
- Cut 2 each of ornaments A, B, C, and D.
- Cut 3 each of ornaments E, F, G, and H.

2. Refer to the photo (page 24) as you appliqué the pieces to the borders.

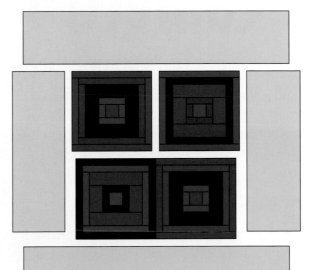

Block and border assembly

Finishing

1. Layer the table topper with batting and backing. Baste or pin.

2. Quilt as desired and bind.

Confetti Table Topper

FINISHED TABLE TOPPER SIZE: 40½″ × 40½″

Quilted by Diane Minkley of Patched Works, Inc.

Add some sparkle to your table with this simple appliquéd-border table topper. Perfect for the holiday festivities.

Materials

- 1¼ yards black for appliqué background
- ½ yard total assorted brights for appliqué pieces
- 1 yard paper-backed fusible web
- 2⅝ yards for backing and binding
- 45″ × 45″ batting

Cutting

CUT FROM THE BLACK

1 square 40½″ × 40½″ for the appliqué background

Appliquéing

Refer to Appliqué (page 8) as needed. Appliqué patterns are on pullout page P4.

1. Using the appliqué patterns:

- Cut 9 each of appliqué pieces 1 through 4.

2. Refer to the photo (page 28) as you appliqué all the pieces to the background.

Finishing

1. Layer the table topper with batting and backing. Baste or pin.

2. Quilt as desired and bind.

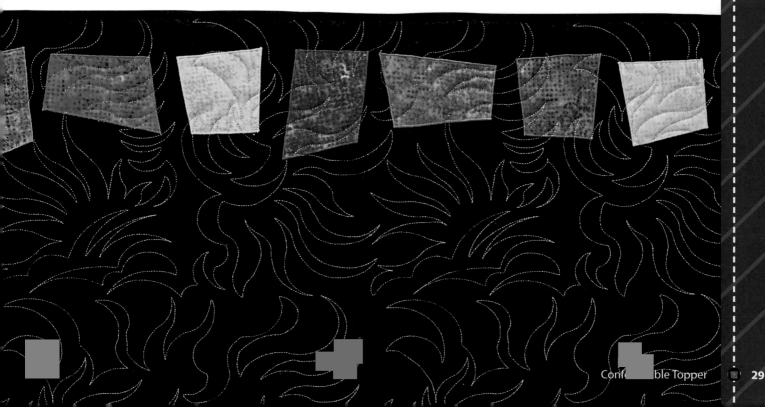

Dots and Stripes Runner

FINISHED RUNNER SIZE:

20½″ × 50½″

Quilted by Diane Minkley of Patched Works, Inc.

It's all about dots and stripes in this easy-to-piece runner with a contemporary look.

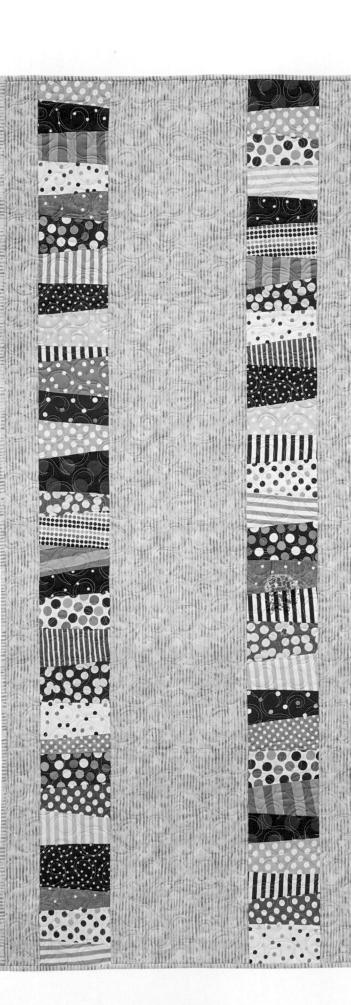

A Merry Christmas with Kim Schaefer

Materials

- 1½ yards light green for runner center, borders, and backing
- 1 yard total assorted dots and stripes for pieced rows
- 25″ × 55″ batting
- ⅓ yard for binding

Cutting

CUT FROM THE LIGHT GREEN

1 lengthwise strip 8½″ × 50½″

2 lengthwise strips 2½″ × 50½″

CUT FROM THE ASSORTED DOTS AND STRIPES

59 rectangles 3½″ × 5½″

Piecing

1. Arrange and sew together the rectangles in random order at different angles. Each pieced row should measure at least 50½″ in length. Press. Make 2 rows.

2. Trim the pieced rows to 4½″ × 50½″.

Putting It All Together

1. Refer to the putting it all together diagram (below) as you sew the center piece between the pieced rows. Press.

2. Sew the borders to the runner. Press.

Finishing

1. Layer the runner with batting and backing. Baste or pin.

2. Quilt as desired and bind.

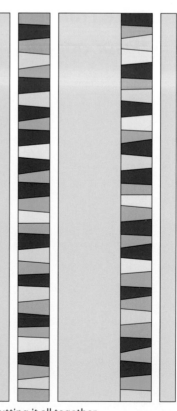

Piece rectangles at different angles. Make 2 rows.

Putting it all together

Holiday Runner

FINISHED RUNNER SIZE:
20½″ × 60½″

Quilted by Diane Minkley of
Patched Works, Inc.

*Traditional reds and
greens are used to
create this simple
pieced runner with
classic appeal.*

Materials

- ½ yard total assorted green solids for pieced rows
- 1 yard red print for runner center and ends
- 25″ × 65″ batting
- 1⅞ yards for backing and binding

Cutting

CUT FROM THE ASSORTED GREEN SOLIDS

80 squares 2½″ × 2½″

CUT FROM THE RED PRINT

1 rectangle 20½″ × 32½″

2 rectangles 20½″ × 6½″

Piecing

1. Arrange and sew together 8 rows of 10 squares each. Press.

2. Sew together 2 sets of 4 rows each. Press.

Putting It All Together

Refer to the putting it all together diagram (right) as you sew together the runner. Press.

Finishing

1. Layer the runner with batting and backing. Baste or pin.

2. Quilt as desired and bind.

Putting it all together

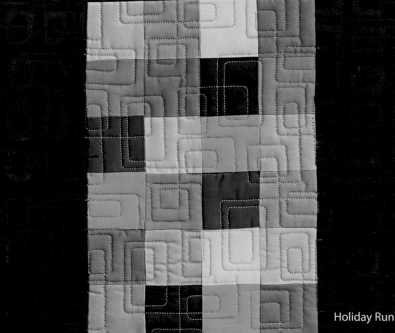

Losing My Head Wall Quilt

FINISHED WALL QUILT SIZE: 24½″ × 32½″

Quilted by Diane Minkley of Patched Works, Inc.

Decorate your wall or door for the winter season with this whimsical snowman quilt. Machine appliqué using paper-backed fusible web makes this quilt go together quickly and easily.

Materials

- ½ yard gray for appliqué background

- ⅛ yard red for inner border

- ½ yard total assorted brights for pieced border

- ½ yard light for snowman

- ¼ yard black for neck, arms, buttons, eyes, legs, and cardinal faces

- ¼ yard black print for boots

- Scrap of orange for nose

- Scraps of 2 reds for cardinal bodies and wings

- Scrap of yellow for cardinal beaks

- 1 yard paper-backed fusible web

- 1¼ yards for backing and binding

- 28″ × 36″ batting

- Black permanent marker for smile

Cutting

CUT FROM THE GRAY

1 rectangle 15½″ × 23½″ for the appliqué background

CUT FROM THE RED

2 strips 1″ × 23½″ for the 2 side inner borders

2 strips 1″ × 16½″ for the top and bottom inner borders

CUT FROM THE ASSORTED BRIGHTS

24 squares 4½″ × 4½″ for the pieced borders

Piecing

1. Sew the 2 side inner borders to the background. Press toward the borders.

2. Sew the top and bottom inner borders to the background. Press.

3. Sew together 4 rows of 6 squares each for the outer borders. Press.

4. Sew the 2 side pieced borders to the quilt top. Press.

5. Sew the top and bottom pieced borders to the quilt top. Press.

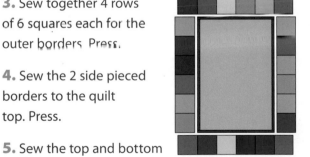
Piece background and borders

Appliquéing

Refer to Appliqué (page 8) as needed. Appliqué patterns are on pullout page P2.

1. Using the appliqué patterns:

- Cut 1 each of appliqué pieces 1 through 9.

- Cut 2 of appliqué piece 10.

- Cut 1 each and 1 each reverse of appliqué pieces 11 through 16.

2. Refer to the putting it all together diagram (below) as you appliqué the pieces to the quilt top.

Finishing

1. Layer the quilt top with batting and backing. Baste or pin.

2. Quilt as desired and bind.

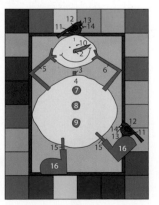
Putting it all together

The Christmas Line Wall Quilt

FINISHED WALL QUILT SIZE: 75½″ × 27½″

Quilted by Diane Minkley of Patched Works, Inc.

Spruce up a wall or mantel with Santa and his dancing reindeer. This whimsical wall quilt has a light background and a brightly colored pieced border for a fresh look.

Materials

- 2 yards light for appliqué background and pieced border

- ½ yard total assorted brights for pieced border, ornaments, and belt buckle

- ⅛ yard tan for antlers

- ½ yard total assorted browns for reindeer

- ⅛ yard light for reindeer bellies

- ⅓ yard red for Santa suit and hat

- ⅛ yard black for hooves, ornament hangers, noses, mittens, belt, and boots

- 2½ yards paper-backed fusible web

- 80″ × 32″ batting

- 2½ yards for backing and binding

- 10 small black buttons for eyes

Cutting

CUT FROM THE LIGHT

1 rectangle 69½″ × 21½″ for the appliqué background

32 squares 3½″ × 3½″ for the pieced border

CUT FROM THE ASSORTED BRIGHTS

32 squares 3½″ × 3½″ for the pieced border

Appliquéing

Refer to Appliqué (page 8) as needed. Appliqué patterns are on pullout page P1 and P3.

1. Using the appliqué patterns:

- Cut 4 each of appliqué pieces 2 through 9.

- Cut 12 of appliqué piece 10.

- Cut 1 each of appliqué pieces 11 through 28.

- Cut a strip ⅛″ wide × 15″. Subcut at varying lengths for 12 ornament hangers.

2. Refer to the Christmas Line Tree Skirt panel diagrams (page 13) for placement of the pieces. Appliqué the pieces to the background.

Piecing

1. Refer to the border assembly diagram as you arrange and sew together 2 rows of 7 squares each for the 2 side pieced borders.

2. Sew the 2 side borders to the quilt top. Press.

3. Arrange and sew together 2 rows of 25 squares each for the top and bottom pieced borders.

4. Sew the top and bottom borders to the quilt top. Press.

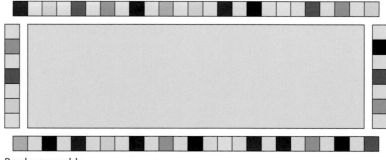

Border assembly

Finishing

1. Layer the quilt top with batting and backing. Baste or pin.

2. Quilt as desired and bind.

Double Wrap Lap Quilt

FINISHED BLOCK SIZE: 9″ × 9″ • **FINISHED LAP QUILT SIZE:** 51½″ × 71½″

Quilted by Diane Minkley of Patched Works, Inc.

Cuddle up under this bright and festive lap quilt and enjoy the holiday season.

Materials

- 1½ yards total assorted reds for pieced blocks
- 1½ yards total assorted greens for pieced blocks
- 2¼ yards light for pieced blocks and lattice
- 4¼ yards for backing and binding
- 56″ × 76″ batting

Cutting

Note: The pieces for each matching set of squares and rectangles are listed together.

CUT FROM THE ASSORTED REDS

18 squares 3½″ × 3½″

68 squares 2½″ × 2½″ and 68 rectangles 2½″ × 4½″ (Use 4 of each size for each block.)

CUT FROM THE ASSORTED GREENS

17 squares 3½″ × 3½″

72 squares 2½″ × 2½″ and 72 rectangles 2½″ × 4½″ (Use 4 of each size for each block.)

CUT FROM THE LIGHT

70 rectangles 1½″ × 3½″ and 70 rectangles 1½″ × 5½″ (Use 2 of each size for each block.)

140 rectangles 1½″ × 2½″ (Use 4 for each block.)

42 rectangles 1½″ × 9½″ for vertical lattice

11 strips 1½″ × width of fabric. Sew end to end. Then cut 8 pieces 1½″ × 51½″ for the horizontal lattice and top and bottom borders.

Piecing

1. Piece the A blocks as shown. Press the seams toward the darker fabrics. Make 18 blocks.

2. Piece the B blocks as shown. Press the seams toward the darker fabrics. Make 17 blocks.

Step 1

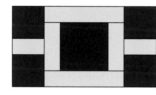

Step 2

Step 1

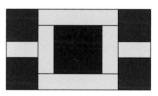

Step 2

Step 3

Step 4

Step 3

Step 4

Step 5

Step 5

Step 6

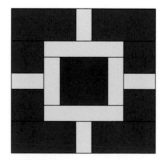

Step 6

A Merry Christmas with Kim Schaefer

Putting It All Together

1. Refer to the putting it all together diagram (below) as you arrange the blocks in 7 rows of 5 blocks each, alternating A and B blocks.

2. Sew the vertical lattice pieces between the blocks and at the ends of the rows. Press toward the blocks.

3. Sew the horizontal lattice pieces between the rows. Press toward the blocks.

4. Sew the top and bottom borders to the quilt. Press.

Finishing

1. Layer the quilt top with batting and backing. Baste or pin.

2. Quilt as desired and bind.

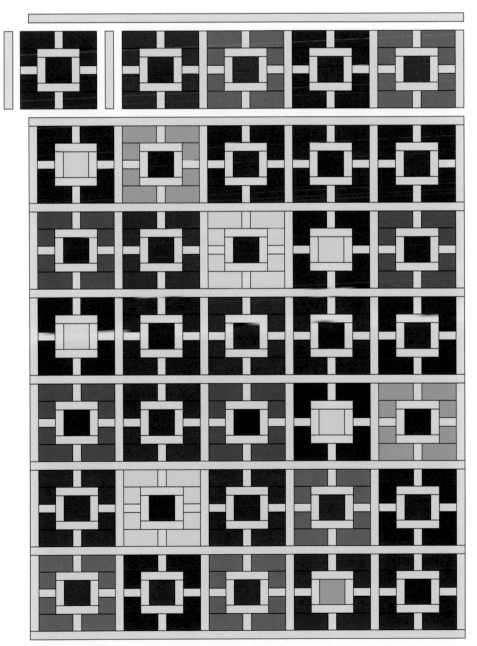

Putting it all together

Ornament Wreath

FINISHED WREATH SIZE: 22″ in diameter

Brighten your wall or door with one of these fun-to-make, no-sew wreaths.

Materials

- 1 Styrofoam wreath form, 18″ in diameter
- 92 Styrofoam balls, 2″ in diameter
- ⅔ yards green for wrapping the wreath
- 2 yards total assorted brights for wrapping the balls
- Fabric glue

Cutting

CUT FROM THE GREEN

13 strips 1½″ × width of fabric

CUT FROM THE ASSORTED BRIGHTS

138 strips ½″ × width of fabric

Putting It All Together

1. Wrap the wreath with the green fabric strips. Glue the ends in place.

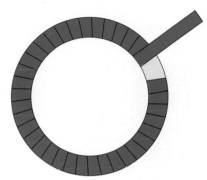

Wrap wreath.

2. Wrap the Styrofoam balls with the bright ½″ strips, overlapping the strips slightly. Glue the ends in place. Allow 1½ strips per ball.

3. Arrange and glue the balls to the wreath form.

Holly Berry Wreath

FINISHED WREATH SIZE: 19˝ in diameter

A Merry Christmas with Kim Schaefer

Materials

- 1 Styrofoam wreath form, 18″ in diameter
- ⅔ yard green for wrapping the wreath
- 2 yards total assorted greens for holly leaves
- ⅛ yard total assorted reds for berries
- 2 yards fast2fuse
- Fabric glue
- Template plastic

Cutting

CUT FROM THE GREEN

13 strips 1½″ × width of fabric

Putting It All Together

Patterns are on pullout page P4.

1. Wrap the wreath with the green fabric strips. Glue the ends in place.

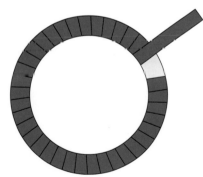

Wrap wreath.

2. Using the patterns, make plastic templates of pattern pieces 1 through 4.

3. Sandwich the fast2fuse between the wrong sides of the assorted greens. Press and fuse the fabrics to the fast2fuse.

4. Trace and cut 32 of pattern piece 1.

5. Sandwich the fast2fuse between the wrong sides of the assorted reds. Press and fuse the fabrics to the fast2fuse.

6. Trace and cut 4 of pattern piece 2. Trace and cut 5 of pattern piece 3. Trace and cut 6 of pattern piece 4.

7. Arrange the leaves and berries on the wreath form. Glue everything in place.

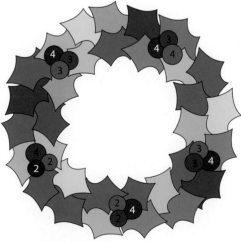

Putting it all together

Merry Christmas Banner

FINISHED BANNER SIZE: 66″ × 20″

Greet family and guests alike with an easy-to-make banner.

A Merry Christmas with Kim Schaefer

Materials

- 14 fat quarters of assorted greens for letter backgrounds and backing
- ¾ yard total assorted reds for letters
- 1¾ yards fast2fuse
- 14 buttons
- 6 yards green grosgrain ribbon
- 1 yard paper-backed fusible web
- 8½″ × 8½″ template plastic

Cutting

CUT FROM THE ASSORTED GREENS

2 squares 8½″ × 8½″ from each of the 14 fat quarters for the letter backgrounds

CUT FROM THE FAST2FUSE

14 squares 8½″ × 8½″

Putting It All Together

Refer to Appliqué (page 8) as needed. Circle and appliqué patterns are on pullout pages P1 and P3.

1. Sandwich the fast2fuse squares between the green squares. Press and fuse the fabrics to the fast2fuse.

2. Make a plastic template of pattern piece 1. Trace and cut 14 of pattern piece 1 from the green squares.

3. Trace and cut the letter pattern pieces from the assorted reds.

4. Refer to the photo (page 46) as you fuse the pieces to the circles.

5. Attach the circles to the grosgrain ribbon with the buttons, as shown.

6. Tie the ribbons together with a loop knot.

Happy Holidays Banner

FINISHED BANNER SIZE: 66″ × 20″

Add holiday cheer with a holiday banner.

A Merry Christmas with Kim Schaefer

Materials

- 1⅔ yards black for letter backgrounds
- ¾ yard total assorted brights for letters
- 1⅔ yards fast2fuse
- 13 buttons
- 6 yards black grosgrain ribbon
- 1 yard paper-backed fusible web
- 8½″ × 8½″ template plastic

Putting It All Together

Refer to Appliqué (page 8) as needed. Circle and appliqué patterns are on pullout out pages P1 and P3.

1. Sandwich the fast2fuse between wrong sides of the black fabric. Press and fuse the fabric to the fast2fuse.

2. Make a plastic template of pattern piece 1. Trace and cut 13 of pattern piece 1 from the black.

3. Trace and cut the letter pattern pieces from the assorted brights.

4. Refer to the photo (page 48) as you fuse the pieces to the circles.

5. Attach the circles to the grosgrain ribbon with the buttons, as shown.

6. Tie the ribbons together with a loop knot.

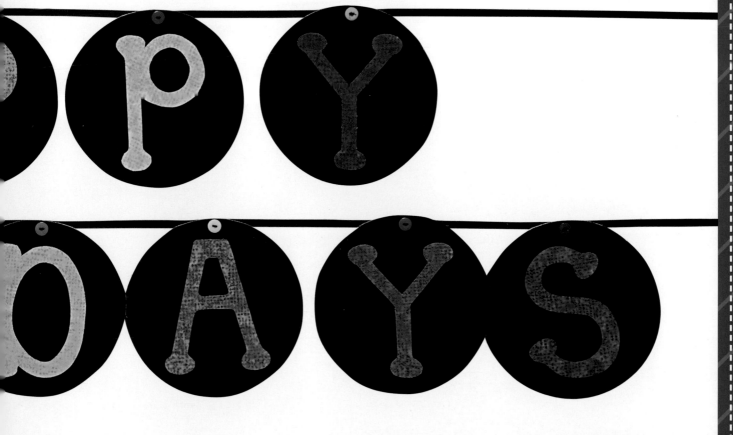

Coasters

FINISHED COASTER SIZE: 4″ round

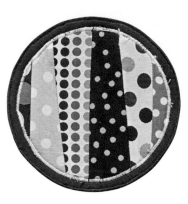

Coasters are simple and fun to make and add to your holiday decor. Choose from eight different designs. They make a great gift-giving idea.

Materials
(per coaster)

- 2 fabric squares 4½″ × 4½″ for coaster front and back

- 1 fabric square 4″ × 4″ for appliqué background

- Assorted scraps for appliqué pieces and pieced coaster

- 1 square 4½″ × 4½″ fast2fuse

- Template plastic

- ⅛ yard paper-backed fusible web

Make the Coaster

Circle pattern is on pullout page P4.

1. Sandwich the fast2fuse squares between the wrong sides of the coaster front and back squares. Press and fuse the fabrics to the fast2fuse square.

2. Make a plastic template of pattern piece 1. Trace and cut 1 of pattern piece 1.

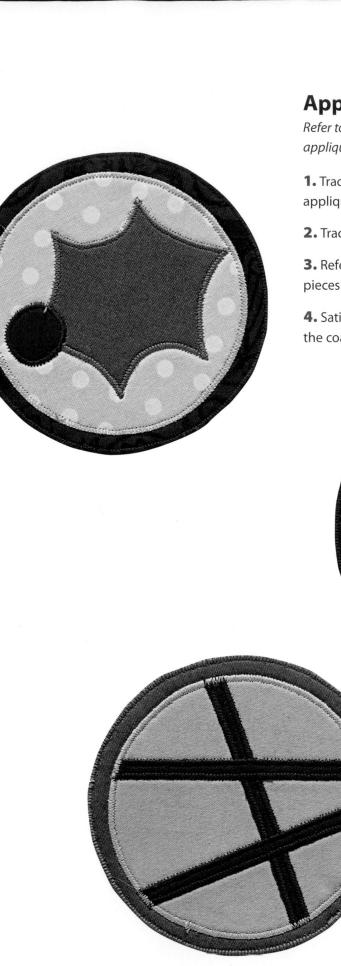

Appliquéd Coaster

Refer to Appliqué (page 8) as needed. Circle and appliqué patterns are on pullout page P4.

1. Trace and cut 1 of pattern piece 2 for the appliqué background.

2. Trace and cut the appliqué pattern pieces.

3. Refer to the photos as you appliqué the pieces to the coaster.

4. Satin stitch around the outside edge of the coaster.

Pieced Coaster

1. Cut 6 strips 1½″ × 4″ from your chosen fabrics.

2. Arrange and sew together the strips at random angles.

3. Trace 1 of pattern piece 2. Fuse it to the back of the pieced strips. Cut on the traced line.

4. Press and fuse to the coaster front.

5. Satin stitch around the pieced circle and the outside edge of the coaster.

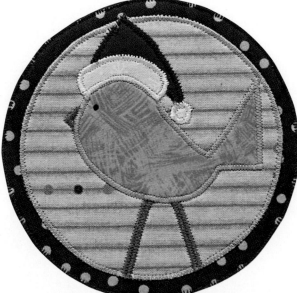

Gift Tags

FINISHED GIFT TAG SIZE: 4″ × 2″

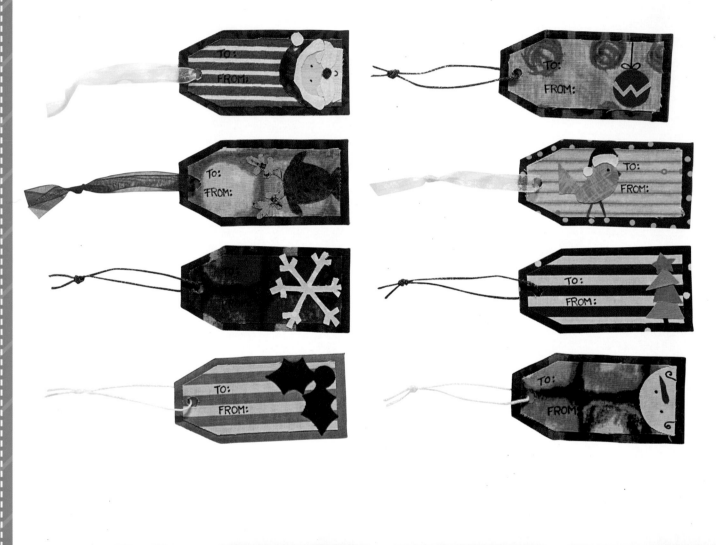

Personalize your gifts with these easy-to-make, no-sew gift tags.

Materials
(per gift tag)

Makes 1 gift tag.

- 2 fabric rectangles 2½″ × 4½″ for gift tag front and back
- 1 fabric rectangle 2″ × 4″ for appliqué background
- Assorted scraps for appliqué pieces
- 1 rectangle 2½″ × 4½″ fast2fuse
- Template plastic
- ⅓ yard ribbon or cording

Putting It All Together

Refer to Appliqué (page 8) as needed. Gift tag and appliqué patterns are on pullout page P4.

1. Sandwich the fast2fuse rectangle between the wrong sides of the front and back. Press and fuse the fabric to the fast2fuse rectangle.

2. Make a plastic template of pattern piece 1. Trace and cut the gift tag.

3. Make a plastic template of pattern piece 2. Trace and cut the appliqué background. Fuse it to the gift tag.

4. Using sharp scissors, cut the hole in the gift tag.

5. Trace and cut the appliqué pieces.

6. Refer to the photos as you fuse the pieces to the background.

Squares Pillow

FINISHED PILLOW SIZE: 16″ × 16″ square

Materials

- ⅔ yard total assorted green solids for pieced background
- ½ yard total assorted red solids for raw-edge appliqué squares
- 2 each 16½″ × 16½″ batting
- 16″ × 16″ pillow form
- ⅞ yard paper-backed fusible web
- Pinking shears

Cutting

CUT FROM THE ASSORTED GREENS

32 squares 4½″ × 4½″

CUT FROM THE ASSORTED REDS

32 squares 3½″ × 3½″

CUT FROM THE FUSIBLE WEB

32 squares 3½″ × 3½″

Putting It All Together

1. Fuse the paper-backed fusible web squares to the backs of the red squares.

2. Use pinking shears to cut the outside edges of the red squares.

3. Peel off the paper backing from the red squares.

4. Center and fuse the red squares onto the green background squares.

5. Arrange and sew together 2 sets of 4 rows of 4 squares each.

6. Sew together the rows to form the pillow front and back. Press.

7. Layer the batting behind the pillow front and back.

8. Quilt as desired.

Putting it all together

Finishing

1. Place the pillow front and back right sides together.

2. Sew around the outside edges, leaving an 8″ opening at the bottom.

3. Trim the corners. Then turn the pillow cover right side out. Place the pillow form inside the pillow cover through the opening. Hand stitch the opening closed.

Open

Stitch pillow front to back, leaving opening at bottom.

Patched Pillow

FINISHED PILLOW SIZE: 16″ × 16″

Materials

- ⅜ yard white for lattice
- ⅜ yard total assorted red and green prints for piecing
- 2 each 16½″ × 16½″ batting
- 16″ × 16″ pillow form

Cutting

CUT FROM THE WHITE

12 rectangles 1½″ × 16½″

28 rectangles 1½″ × 2½″

CUT FROM THE ASSORTED RED AND GREEN PRINTS

2 rectangles 2½″ × 1½″

6 squares 2½″ × 2½″

12 rectangles 2½″ × 3½″

10 rectangles 2½″ × 4½″

6 rectangles 2½″ × 5½″

2 rectangles 2½″ × 6½″

Putting It All Together

1. Refer to the putting it all together diagram (right) as you sew the vertical lattice pieces between the assorted squares and rectangles to form each pieced row for the pillow front and back. Press.

2. Sew the horizontal lattice pieces between the pieced strips for the pillow front and back. Press.

3. Layer the batting behind the pillow front and back.

4. Quilt as desired.

Finishing

Refer to Squares Pillow, Finishing (page 57) to complete the pillow.

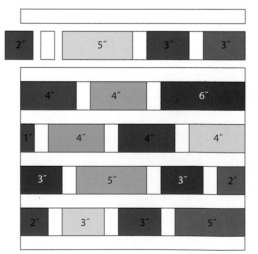

Putting it all together

Side Stripes Pillow

FINISHED PILLOW SIZE: 16″ × 16″

Materials

- ¼ yard light green for pillow center
- ⅔ yard total assorted reds for pieced rows
- ¼ yard dark green for side borders
- 2 each 16½″ × 16½″ batting
- 16″ × 16″ pillow form

Cutting

CUT FROM THE LIGHT GREEN

2 rectangles 6½″ × 16½″

CUT FROM THE ASSORTED REDS

42 rectangles 2″ × 4½″

42 rectangles 1½″ × 4½″

CUT FROM THE DARK GREEN

4 rectangles 2½″ × 16½″

Putting It All Together

1. Refer to the putting it all together diagram (below) as you join the center, pieced rows, and side borders for the pillow front and back.

2. Layer the batting behind the pillow front and back.

3. Quilt as desired.

Finishing

Refer to Squares Pillow, Finishing (page 57) to complete the pillow.

Piecing

1. Refer to the Dots and Stripes Table Runner, Piecing (page 31) as you arrange and sew together the red rectangles in random order at different angles. Make 4 rows. Each row should measure at least 16½″ in length. Press.

2. Trim the rows to 3½″ × 16½″.

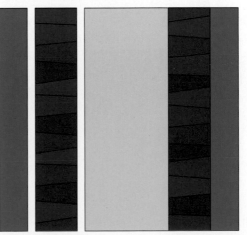

Putting it all together

Quilted Circles Pillow

FINISHED PILLOW SIZE: 16″ × 16″

Materials

- ½ yard red for pillow front and back

- 2 each 16½″ × 16½″ batting

- 16″ × 16″ pillow form

- Erasable fabric marker

Cutting

CUT FROM THE RED

2 squares 16½″ × 16½″

2. Layer the batting behind the pillow front and back.

3. Quilt circles or other patterns as desired.

4. Erase or remove the grid lines, if necessary.

Finishing

Refer to Squares Pillow, Finishing (page 57) to complete the pillow.

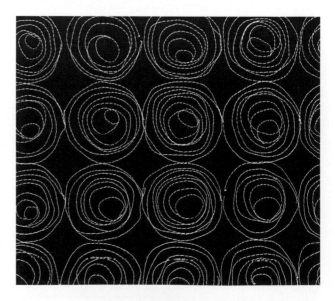

Putting It All Together

1. Use an erasable fabric marker to draw a grid on the pillow front and back.

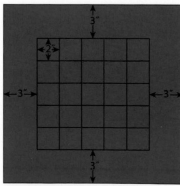

Draw grid on pillow front and back.

Ornament Tree

FINISHED TREE SIZE:

15½″ base × 29″ height

This no-sew tree is fun to make and will add a modern look to your holiday decor.

Materials

- 1 piece of wood
  $\frac{3}{4}'' \times 2\frac{1}{2}'' \times 8'$ for frame

- 3 Styrofoam balls,
  4″ in diameter

- 9 Styrofoam balls,
  3″ in diameter

- 12 Styrofoam balls,
  2″ in diameter

- 1 yard total assorted greens
  for Styrofoam balls

- Fabric glue

- 1 can white satin spray paint

Cutting

**CUT FROM THE
ASSORTED GREENS**

18 strips ½″ × width of fabric

22 strips 1″ × width of fabric

Putting It All Together

1. Cut 24″ from the 8′ board. Set aside for the base.

2. Cut the remaining 6′ board in half using a 15° angle cut.

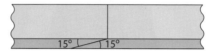

Cut 6′ board in half using 15° angle cut.

3. Glue the 2 angled pieces together as shown.

4. Mark 30″ down each side and measure X for the base.

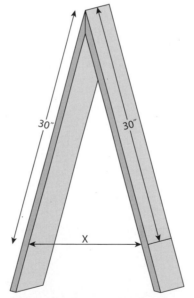

Glue 2 angled pieces together. Measure X for base.

5. Cut the measured distance X from the 24″ remaining board and cut 75° angles in each end to create the tree base.

6. Glue the base to the 2 sides and trim the extra length from the 2 sides.

7. Spray paint the completed tree form, following the spray can directions.

8. Use the ½″ strips to wrap the 2″ balls. Glue the strip ends in place. Allow 1½ strips per ball.

9. Use the 1″ strips to wrap the 3″ and 4″ balls. Glue the strip ends in place. Allow 1½ strips per 3″ ball and 2½ strips per 4″ ball.

10. Arrange the balls inside the wooden tree form. Glue the balls in place.

The tree can be used free standing or hung on a wall.

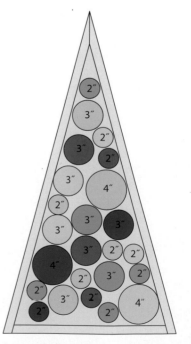

Putting it all together

About the Author

KIM SCHAEFER began sewing at an early age and was quilting seriously by the late 1980s. Her early quilting career included designing and producing small quilts for craft shows and shops across the country.

In 1986, Kim founded Little Quilt Company, a pattern company focused on designing a variety of small, fun-to-make projects.

In addition to designing quilt patterns, Kim is a best-selling author for C&T Publishing. Kim also designs fabric for Andover Fabrics.

Kim lives with her family in southeastern Wisconsin.

For more information on Little Quilt Company, please visit littlequiltcompany.com, which offers Kim's entire collection of patterns, books, and fabrics.

Little Quilt Company's Facebook page has posts about new patterns, books, and fabrics, as well as an occasional peek at Kim's latest work.

Also by Kim Schaefer

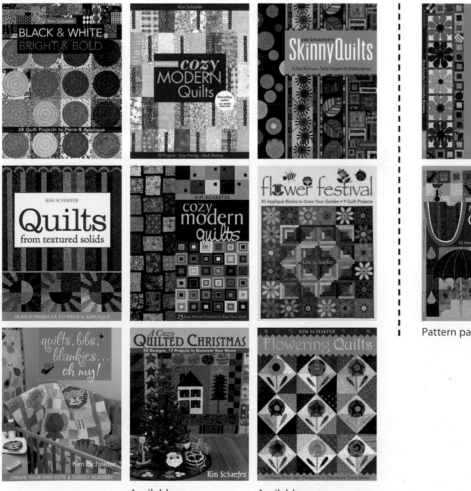

Pattern packs

Available as an eBook only

Available as an eBook only

746.46
SCH

Great Titles *from* C&T PUBLISHING & **stash**BOOKS.

Available at your local retailer or **ctpub.com** *or* **800-284-1114**